Living in the Light

in the

Light

Daily Reflections,
Prayers, and Practices
for Advent

Cycles A, B, & C

Rev. Warren J. Savage
Mary Ann McSweeny

Liguori

ONE LIGUORI DRIVE
LIGUORI MO 63057-9999
314.464.2500

Imprimi Potest:
Richard Thibodeau, C.SS.R.
Provincial, Denver Province
The Redemptorists

Imprimatur:
Most Reverend Michael J. Sheridan
Auxiliary Bishop, Archdiocese of St. Louis

ISBN 0-7648-0148-1
Library of Congress Catalog Card Number: 97-74321

Scripture quotations are from the *New American Bible*,
copyright © 1970 by the Confraternity of Christian
Doctrine, 3211 Fourth Street N.E., Washington, DC
20017-1194, and are used with permission. All rights
reserved.

Cover design by Wendy Barnes

Lent:
A Time to Walk in the Light

Lent, the season of repentance, is upon us. Traditionally, Lent is a time for us to reflect upon life and our relationship with God and with others. It is also an opportunity for us to look at those areas of our lives that need to be changed if we are to become more responsible and sensible in light of our relationship with Jesus Christ, the Light of the world.

This is the season to assess our attitude toward life, to get in touch with our feelings, and to see how we balance the two in our day-to-day experiences. This is the season to create a personal spirituality and daily prayer life that looks at our addictive and destructive behaviors to find ways to correct and overcome them.

Lent is our sacred time. It is a time to do serious, personal work toward becoming holy, integrated persons—our ultimate aim being inner peace and strength to love God, neighbor, and self as a way of life.

The disciplines of Lent include *fasting, prayer,* and *almsgiving.* These disciplines find their meaning in the context of the poor, alienated, and marginalized people throughout our community, nation, and world. The purpose of fasting, prayer, and almsgiving is to unite us more closely to the poor, thus inspiring us to become more sensitive to their needs and more responsible for the establishment of justice and peace.

The reflections that follow are meant to foster a spirit of personal prayer, reflection, and conversion. In fasting, we struggle to come to terms with those things in life that cause inner chaos, conflict, and division. We *fast* from negativity and embrace what we need to become holy, integrated persons in community. In prayer we long for unity among all God's people. We *pray* for a greater understanding of the common ground upon which we stand, and a deeper appreciation of the diversity of God's creation. In almsgiving we *make a concrete commitment* to justice and peace, deliberately choosing a plan of action that improves the quality of life and our relationships with others.

It is hoped that at the end of this Lenten retreat we will be more like Christ, our Light, and that our life will be more focused, integrated, and peaceful. The Lord invites us to a change of mind, heart, and spirit. To respond to this invitation, we must be willing to experience a personal conversion to the Christ of peace, love, and compassion. Through fasting, prayer, and almsgiving we can change ourselves and the world in which we live. Let us do our best in the days ahead to become children living in the Light.

Ash Wednesday
Joel 2:12-18; 2 Corinthians 5:20–6:2; Matthew 6:1-6,16-18

Reflection: It is hard for me to do a good deed without wanting to tell someone. Perhaps this is because of the deep fear I have that I am not really a good person, and so I need someone else's approval to feel good about myself. As I learn to trust that I am good and that God loves me in every moment, I will find it less important to seek other people's approval. I will begin to believe the wisdom of my own heart that tells me I am good. I will come to understand that the good I do for others comes out of the truth that the God who is good lives in me. I am a child of God, worthy of having good done to me.

Ponder: Do I parade my religious activities for all to see? How do I pray? In private? in public? in arrogance? in humility? in need? in gratitude? What do I need to change in my life?

Prayer: God, lead me on the path of your Light. Help me to recognize that I am your precious child.

Practice: Today I will fast from seeking approval from others; I will pray for belief in my self-worth; I will perform a good deed in secret.

Thursday after Ash Wednesday
Deuteronomy 30:15-20; Luke 9:22-25

Reflection: It is not easy to get up every day and face the world. Some of the burdens in my life seem too heavy to carry: pain, family troubles, death, depression, an unfulfilling job, school-mates who taunt me, illness, teachers who overload me with work, an unappreciative supervisor. When I make a conscious choice every day to put my trust in God's unconditional love for me and to look for joy in every moment, the burdens will not seem so heavy.

Ponder: Do I look on the negative side of things or on the positive side? Do I choose joy over gloom in my everyday life? Do I hold fast to God? Do I think that I'm the only person who suffers in life? Is Jesus on the cross a source of help for me?

Prayer: God, lead me on the path of your Light. Help me to look for the positive in my life.

Practice: Today I will fast from being a negative person; I will pray for the strength to be hopeful in a difficult moment; I will consciously choose to be happy.

Friday after Ash Wednesday
Isaiah 58:1-9; Matthew 9:14-15

Reflection: Perhaps I am stuck in certain routines or patterns of speech or thought. Perhaps I feel like my life is out of control, dull, or narrow. When I am open to new ways of action, thought, and speech, I change the patterns that keep me from living a life of serenity and interest. Listening to other people, joining a support group, participating in a prayer group, reading spiritual literature, seeking counseling: all of these can be healthy sources of introducing flexibility into my life, allowing me to experience life more fully.

Ponder: Is it hard for me to change? Are there certain values I need to keep even when things change? when times change? Are there certain values I need to reassess? How can I bring about and respect change?

Prayer: God, lead me on the path of your Light. Help me to broaden my perspective.

Practice: Today I will fast from narrow-mindedness; I will pray for tolerance; I will read about the culture and traditions of another person.

Saturday after Ash Wednesday
Isaiah 58:9-14; Luke 5:27-32

Reflection: When I spend a lot of time with people who are negative, unjust, and judgmental, I tend to think, speak, and act in negative, unjust, and judgmental ways myself. When I choose the company of people who are loving, tolerant, and respectful, I tend to think, speak, and act in loving, tolerant, and respectful ways myself.

Ponder: Would I want to be one of Levi's dinner guests? Do I consider myself too healthy to need Jesus? How would I respond if I heard Jesus say, "Follow me"? Do I watch what I eat and drink? Do I need a change of heart?

Prayer: God, lead me on the path of your Light. Help me to seek healthy relationships.

Practice: Today I will fast from unhealthy associations; I will pray for a healthy attitude; I will spend time with a good friend or companion.

The First Week of Lent

Cycle A
Led by the Spirit of Love

"Jesus was led into the desert by the Spirit to be tempted by the devil. He fasted forty days and forty nights, and afterward was hungry" (Matthew 4:1-2).

It seems to be a strange starting point for us, but upon reflection we begin to understand that the desert is symbolic of all that is barren, lifeless, cold, and dry. On another level we become aware of the truth that the human condition, at times, feels like a desert experience.

We journey with Jesus into the desert to face all that is barren, lifeless, cold, and dry within us. This is the challenge we face this week as we attempt to explore the meaning of life in light of Jesus' battle with the devil in the desert. We remember how the Israelites struggled to survive in the desert for forty years until they reached the Promised Land. In recent times we have witnessed thousands of people dying from famine and disease in the deserts of Africa. We have been horrified by the killing of innocent people in war-torn parts of the world. And we have encountered those who live in the desert of loneliness, despair, poverty, and illness.

There is a temptation in the world to take advantage of all that is weak and poor. There is a temptation on our part to be self-centered in pursuit of our own needs, to be irresponsible and act unjustly in our community, and to be apathetic and ignore the needs of our sisters and brothers.

As we begin our Lenten journey, we become more aware of our frail human condition and our need for God's help in the midst of our desert storms and hungers.

First Sunday of Lent—Cycle A
Genesis 2:7-9;3:1-7; Romans 5:12-19; Matthew 4:1-11

Reflection: By going into the desert with Jesus I have an opportunity to deepen my personal commitment to the Lord and to reexamine my relationship with God and my neighbors. I remember that I am created in love that I might fill the world with God's love. It is the spirit of love that will ultimately change and transform my desert experiences.

Ponder: What temptations do I struggle with? Where is my life barren and desert-like? Can I trust that God will support me in my desert experiences? Do I call on God in times of need?

Prayer: God, lead me by the Spirit of your love that I may safely walk through the desert areas of my life.

Practice: This week I will fast from self-centeredness; I will pray for a greater sense of personal responsibility; I will give loving service to the poor and needy in our community.

Cycle B
Good News for the World

"After John's arrest, Jesus appeared in Galilee, proclaiming God's good news: 'This is the time of fulfillment. The reign of God is at hand! Reform your lives, and believe in the good news'"(Mark 1:14-15).

Jesus makes an announcement to the whole world and invites each of us to accept a personal challenge: to reform our lives and believe in the Good News. This timeless proclamation must not be ignored. We need to take seriously the call to reshape our lives in light of God's unconditional love.

Our whole world would be a better place if we all made a commitment to love others, especially those we dislike. There is no greater sense of fulfillment than that of knowing and experiencing the unconditional love of another person. The human wasteland is filled with people who long to be recognized, accepted, and affirmed. There is a deep hunger and thirst in people's lives for genuine love, compassion, and peace.

During these next several weeks, we reflect on the meaning of God's love in our lives. Have we done our best to love others as God has loved us? Why are we afraid to love and be loved? Do we believe that love can and does make a difference in life? Do we trust that love can heal our pain, restore broken relationships, and forgive the wrongs committed against us? These probing questions open the door to a deeper awareness of God's Spirit within us that leads us to a new understanding of our purpose and mission in life. We reform our lives and believe in the Good News of God's love, thus restoring balance, harmony, and peace in a fragile world.

The stage has been set for us and the script has been proclaimed by the Lord. As followers of Christ we go public with the Good News of love, compassion, and peace. We believe that God has given us what we need to reform the face of this earth. We have great hope: "This is the time of fulfillment. The reign of God is at hand!"

First Sunday of Lent—Cycle B
Genesis 9:8-15; 1 Peter 3:18-22; Mark 1:12-15

Reflection: The Spirit of God is leading me out of my old ways of thinking and old patterns of behavior to new challenges and opportunities. I am being called to move beyond inaction and to take a stand against all forms of greed, selfishness, hatred, disrespect, and violence. The Spirit of God is awakening within me a desire to share my gifts and talents for the common good. The Spirit of God is liberating me from my fears and doubts and giving me the courage to be an agent of change. The Spirit of God is reminding me that as a child of God I have Good News to share with the world.

Ponder: Is my conscience irreproachable? Do I have any spiritual stains that need to be cleansed? Have I ever spent time in a spiritual desert? Am I ready to reform my life? Do I believe the reign of God is at hand? Do I believe in the Good News of God's love for me and the world?

Prayer: God, lead me by the Spirit of your love that I may share your Good News of love, peace, and compassion with others.

Practice: This week I will fast from pride; I will pray to be open to a change of mind and heart; I will speak out against disrespect, violence, and prejudice.

Cycle C
Seizing Opportunities

"Jesus, full of the Holy Spirit, returned from the Jordan and was led by the Spirit into the desert for forty days, where he was tempted by the devil" (Luke 4:1-2).

We are surrounded by temptations. We don't have the strength and the will power to overcome the barrage of voices that call us to feed our addictions, exploit others at any cost, and disregard the sanctity of life. Jesus, too, is tempted; he is confronted by the devil who offers him opportunities to satisfy his hunger, gain power over the whole world, and surrender responsibility for his life to other forces. What appear on the surface to be opportunities for personal and spiritual growth are in reality temptations to disrupt the spiritual heart of humanity that keeps us healthy and holy.

During these forty days of Lent we walk in the desert with the Spirit of God, take a serious look at the many opportunities that come into our lives, and spend sufficient time reflecting on how these opportunities lead us to authentic goodness or lead us away from our true potential as disciples of the Lord.

The bread that is offered to Jesus by the devil is symbolic of our need to be fed because we are basically hungry people. What are our basic hungers and how do we live in a world that has something to feed us every time a perceived need arises? How do we respond to the real hungers for love, peace, justice, liberation, and compassion? How do we become the living bread in a world that refuses to feed the poor?

The power of control and manipulation that the devil offers Jesus is symbolic of the authority that seeks to oppress the weak and vulnerable. How do we deal with our need for control and power over other people's lives? How do we deal with our lives when we are out of control and cause turmoil and division in a variety of ways? There is so much violence throughout the world that we need to disarm our hearts and minds of negative feelings and attitudes and strive to balance the world with love.

During these next forty days, we have the opportunity to enrich the precious gift of life by reaching out to the poor, the vulnerable, and the neglected. We are called to seize every spiritual opportunity to feed the real hungers, to balance the world with love, and to nurture life in all its dimensions. To wake up with a profound appreciation for life can and will make a difference in the lives of others around us. Truly, the Spirit of God will not mislead us.

First Sunday of Lent—Cycle C
Deuteronomy 26:4-10; Romans 10:8-13; Luke 4:1-13

Reflection: The challenge to avoid responsibility, as is offered to Jesus by the devil in the desert, is symbolic of the pervasive mentality to disregard and disrespect the sacredness of human life. All life comes from God and is a precious gift to be treated with dignity and respect. I have no authority to take life into my own hands and play God. Technology has opened up many new and exciting opportunities, but it has also become a replacement for the human need to remain connected to God, the giver and source of life.

Ponder: Has anyone ever oppressed me physically, mentally, emotionally, or spiritually? Do I cry out to God for help in times of need? Does God answer my cry? Do I believe in my heart that God will save me? Do I take advantage of new opportunities to grow closer to God? What temptations do I give in to? What temptations do I resist?

Prayer: God, lead me by the Spirit of your love that I may uphold the sacredness of human life in all its diversity.

Practice: This week I will fast from meddling in other people's affairs; I will pray for the wisdom to know right from wrong; I will give my time, energy, and material goods to enrich the lives of the poor, the vulnerable, and the neglected.

Monday, the First Week of Lent
Leviticus 19:1-2,11-18; Matthew 25:31-46

Reflection: When I am hungry for a kind word and thirsty for recognition, I want to speak kindly and show appreciation to others. When I feel nervous walking into a group of people I don't know well, I want to respond to those who greet me and remember to share the welcome I have received with others. When I feel trapped by sadness or depression, I want to accept comfort from good friends and take the time to ask how my loved ones are doing.

Ponder: What do I hunger for? What do I thirst for? Love? affection? approval? Have I neglected anyone lately? Do I take the time to comfort people in need? Do I cherish the people who love me?

Prayer: God, lead me by the Spirit of your love that I may learn to welcome, feed, clothe, and comfort others with a generous heart.

Practice: Today I will fast from indifference; I will pray for a compassionate heart; I will welcome everyone I meet with a sincere smile.

Tuesday, the First Week of Lent
Isaiah 55:10-11; Matthew 6:7-15

Reflection: Placing my needs and wants in God's hands means I let go of worry and concentrate on making today as peaceful and serene as possible. Although it is hard for me to trust that everything I need today will be provided, I must continue turning my worries over to God with patient and gentle discipline, and with faith in God's loving and merciful care for me.

Ponder: What do I need to pray for today? How can I know and practice God's will? Where in my life has God forgiven me? Why is it difficult for me to accept God's forgiveness? Have I forgiven myself? Is there someone I need to forgive?

Prayer: God, lead me by the Spirit of your love that I may learn to trust that you will take care of all my needs.

Practice: Today I will fast from worry; I will pray for trust; I will forgive someone who has hurt me.

Wednesday, the First Week of Lent
Jonah 3:1-10; Luke 11:29-32

Reflection: Resisting change expends a lot of physical, mental, emotional, and spiritual energy. When I am struggling with something too big for me to handle, I will remember to turn to God for help to see and understand what I need to change. God is always there to help me when I ask for and am open to change.

Ponder: Is there anything in my life that I need to reform? Am I ready to do what is necessary to let change occur? Can I trust that God is willing to work with and through me? Have I condemned myself for who I am?

Prayer: God, lead me by the Spirit of your love that I may be willing to become a new person.

Practice: Today I will fast from resistance to change; I will pray for a spirit of conversion; I will change something I usually do: the route I take to work, the time I eat lunch, the way I interact with my coworkers.

Thursday, the First Week of Lent
Esther C:12,14-16,23-25; Matthew 7:7-12

Reflection: When pessimism and negativity rule me, I begin to believe that life is meaningless. That's when I need to stay in touch with God, to keep asking and listening for help and guidance. I must cultivate a positive attitude and remember that every day, every moment, I can choose to be happy. God is present to me at all times, ready to show me the way.

Ponder: When I feel alone, do I turn to God? Do I keep in touch with God daily? Do I lack perseverance? Do I know how to ask for what I need?

Prayer: God, lead me by the Spirit of your love that I may keep asking you for help.

Practice: Today I will fast from pessimism; I will pray for a positive attitude; I will make the choice to be happy where I am.

Friday, the First Week of Lent
Ezekiel 18:21-28; Matthew 5:20-26

Reflection: Violence in word or action; betraying trust; holding resentment; violating another's physical, mental, emotional, or spiritual boundaries; gossip: I have done these harmful things. It is hard to believe that God still loves me even though I have done these things. With God's help, however, I can stop harmful behavior and change harmful attitudes. I can acknowledge what I have done and resolve not to act in those ways again. I can become accountable and make amends to those I have harmed. I can also forgive myself, find the courage to keep going toward God, and keep in mind that God loves me—always.

Ponder: Am I aware of my harmful behavior? Do I feel at peace in my interactions with others? Do I get angry at the least transgression? Is there anyone I hold a grudge against? Is my behavior a positive influence on others?

Prayer: God, lead me by the Spirit of your love that I may be gentle toward others.

Practice: Today I will fast from doing harm; I will pray for kindness; I will control my temper.

Saturday, the First Week of Lent
Deuteronomy 26:16-19; Matthew 5:43-48

Reflection: Sometimes I am my own worst enemy. I belittle myself, make fun of myself, judge myself. I don't forgive myself for the mistakes I make. A lack of self-love or a deeply rooted conviction that I am not a worthwhile person usually prompts this kind of reaction, and I carry it into my relationships with others. Because of my low self-esteem, I hide from others and fear that others hate or dislike me. Because of my vulnerability, I often see others as enemies. I become judgmental, sarcastic, and resentful toward people, even those I love.

Ponder: Who are my enemies? Is God my enemy? Do I trust God to love me? Is it hard for me to love God? Do I love myself? Do I treat others with kindness and respect?

Prayer: God, lead me by your Spirit of love that I may make friends, not enemies.

Practice: Today I will fast from shame; I will pray for self-love; I will be a good friend to someone in need.

The Second Week of Lent

Cycle A
The Slow Climb to Change

"Jesus took Peter, James and his brother John and led them up on a high mountain by themselves" (Matthew 17:1).

Last week we began our Lenten journey in the desert. This week we find ourselves on a high mountain, the Mountain of Transfiguration. The mountain is a powerful image symbolizing majesty and freedom. On the mountain we become aware of God, the Creator of the universe. We come to a deeper understanding and awareness of the freedom God gives us to become fully human. The only obstacle holding us back from becoming all that we can become is fear. Perhaps this is why Jesus tells his friends on the mountain, "Do not be afraid."

Jesus takes us up the mountain to show us that we cannot grow without going through an ongoing process of inner change. Throughout life we go through a series of changes and with each change we become new people. Peter, James, and John did not find the climb up the mountain to be easy. They certainly struggled to keep their balance and to not lose heart on the way. Having accomplished the task, they were delighted to be there with the Lord.

This week we look at the mountains that we are afraid to climb. We ask ourselves why we are afraid to go with the Lord to the top of the mountain. We find out why we resist the challenge to change. In that climb, God's majesty and glory will shine in and through us as we are given the freedom to share the glory of God's love, compassion, and peace with others.

After all, we cannot experience the joy and ecstasy of the mountain unless we are willing to make the climb.

Second Sunday of Lent—Cycle A
Genesis 12:1-4; 2 Timothy 1:8-10; Matthew 17:1-9

Reflection: There are moments in my life when I feel like I'm climbing the mountain. I feel like I'm losing my balance. At times like that, I want to give up the struggle. With the Lord, though, I know there is hope. With the Lord I can endure whatever comes my way. With the Lord I am not afraid to change in order to grow in love, peace, and compassion. I can accept the Lord's invitation to be transformed in love.

Ponder: Where do I resist change? When do I resist change? Why do I resist change? How do I resist change? Do I believe that God gives me the power to change? Do I hear God's invitation to change? Do I hear God's call to be a new person? How can I answer?

Prayer: God, help me to keep climbing the mountain of life. Show me the path of courage.

Practice: This week I will fast from fear of God, fear of others, and fear of failure; I will pray for freedom and trust; I will give support to those who find it difficult to overcome the mountain of apathy.

Cycle B
A New Perspective on Life

"Jesus took Peter, James and John off by themselves with him and led them up a high mountain. He was transfigured before their eyes…" (Mark 9:2-3).

Last week we looked at our need to reform our lives and believe in the Good News. We cannot reform our lives, however, without a clear vision of God's plan for us in the world. This week we are caught up in the experience of the Transfiguration, when Jesus shows his friends a new perspective on life.

When we reflect upon the miracle of the Transfiguration, we become aware of our hidden potential as disciples of the Lord. We realize that we have not become all we can become in the power of God's love. We recognize our resistance to become people fully alive in Christ. But Jesus reminds us that when the journey of life is done and all mountains have been climbed, we are embraced by a new life and live in the eternal light of God's love and peace.

With that promise, we enter life's twists and turns, unexpected surprises, and tough situations. As people of faith, we develop an ability to survive and carry on through these experiences. We develop a stronger sense of hope and self-confidence and become more accepting of what comes our way.

This week we look at life with the lens of hope. We examine those areas in life that keep us from seeing goodness in ourselves and in the people around us. We become more optimistic about life and are more willing to take the high road and avoid the pitfalls of disillusionment, despair, self-hatred, and indifference. We help others transform their lives by offering the simple gift of a smile, a warm welcome, a loving embrace. We don't do great things to impress people; rather, we do the little things with great love and compassion.

God has great confidence in us and wants us to be all we can be. God calls us to show others a glimpse of the kingdom by leading them up the mountain so they, too, can experience the transforming power of love and gain a new perspective on life.

Second Sunday of Lent—Cycle B
Genesis 22:1-2,9,10-13,15-18; Romans 8:31-34; Mark 9:2-10

Reflection: It is out of love that Jesus takes his friends up a high mountain and shows them something beautiful and refreshing. It is out of love that God offers me the gift of eternal life. My journey in life can be more meaningful and productive if I keep my eyes fixed on the Risen Lord. My belief in Christ connects me to something that is beyond this world, beyond the highest mountain I can imagine. It is a matter of perspective. If I truly believe that God loves me, then I must believe that this love will never disappoint me. I can walk through life with a profound sense of confident peace, sharing the gift of God's love with others.

Ponder: Do I withhold anything from God? Do I trust God? Do I believe God is for me and not against me? Do I believe that Jesus intercedes on my behalf with God? Have I experienced God's healing transformation in my life? Do I believe I am a beloved child of God?

Prayer: God, help me to keep climbing the mountain of life. Show me the path of love.

Practice: This week I will fast from looking for the gloomy, dark side of situations; I will pray for a clear vision of God's plan for me; I will give encouragement to those who view life with disillusioned eyes.

Cycle C
Alone with God

"Then from the cloud came a voice which said, 'This is my Son, my Chosen One. Listen to him.' When the voice fell silent, Jesus was there alone" (Luke 9:35-36).

Last week we became more aware of the barrage of voices that calls us away from authentic spiritual growth and goodness. This week we discern the voice of God, the voice that constantly reminds us that we are children of God, the voice that constantly affirms us in love.

To do this, we enter aloneness with God. We find a safe space to be with God, where we need not say or do a thing. Of course this might be difficult for some of us because we find it extremely difficult to be alone with ourselves. We feel our attention deficit disorder overcome us while our anxiety increases.

But what really prevents us from sitting quietly and alone with someone who really loves and accepts us as we are? What keeps us from trusting in a loving, merciful, and compassionate God?

After all, there is no real hope for change in our lives if we are not willing to listen to those who care about us the most.

Real change begins with a fundamental awareness that God loves us unconditionally. Jesus takes his friends up the mountain to show them, through his own life, the One who cares about all of humankind. This message is not easily discerned when we have had multiple experiences of rejection, abandonment, and alienation. It is hard to imagine that we are loved when we have been abused and oppressed by others. It is difficult to turn our faces to God when we are afraid and when we hurt so much inside.

This week, we seize the opportunities to find a safe and peaceful place to be alone with God. We remove ourselves from the fast pace of life and the endless noise that drowns out the gentle voice of God. We strive to put more trust in the Lord who desires that we become people fully alive in love, peace, and compassion. Perhaps our being alone with God will help us feel more confident and trusting of our basic goodness and make it easier for us to reach out with love, encouragement, and support to the least of our sisters and brothers.

If we are looking for attention in life, let us remember that God does not have an attention deficit disorder. God focuses on each of us and reminds us that we are a chosen people, a people created in love.

Second Sunday of Lent—Cycle C
Genesis 15:5-12,17-18; Philippians 3:17–4:1; Luke 9:28-36

Reflection: Jesus invites me to go up the mountain and to be with him in the presence of God. With Jesus, I can hear the voice that tells me I will be okay, everything will work out for the good, have no fear, and trust in the One who loved you first. The voice of God gives me the hope and strength I need to carry on in life. Yes, I feel discouraged at times, inadequate, and insecure, but I must never give in to the temptation to stop learning more about God and myself. I grow in self-awareness in the presence of God and in the presence of those who love me.

Ponder: Do I have faith in God's unconditional love for me? Am I afraid to let God's love fill my heart and being? What fears prevent me from letting God love me? Do I enjoy being in God's presence? Is it good for me to spend time with God? Do I enjoy being a favored child of God?

Prayer: God, help me to keep climbing the mountain of life. Show me the path of quiet solitude.

Practice: This week I will fast from having too many obligations; I will pray for a fundamental awareness of God's unconditional love for me; I will seize five minutes of the day to be alone with God.

Monday, the Second Week of Lent
Daniel 9:4-10; Luke 6:36-38

Reflection: I would like to believe that I am all light and goodness but the reality is, there is a shadow side to my character that I must learn to accept. By shining the light of honesty on the anger, fear, shame, and pain in my heart, I am able to accept my brokenness. When I become willing to admit that I am made of light and dark, I stop judging everything and everybody in extremes of good or bad, black or white, rich or poor, free or oppressed. I become more flexible and more loving.

Ponder: Am I quick to judge others? Am I quick to pardon an injury? Do I make haste to ask pardon of someone I have hurt? Do I show compassion to the people around me or do I condemn others by my silence?

Prayer: God, help me to keep climbing the mountain of life. Show me the path of compassion.

Practice: Today I will fast from prejudice; I will pray for compassion; I will show respect to the people around me.

Tuesday, the Second Week of Lent
Isaiah 1:10,16-20; Matthew 23:1-2

Reflection: I talk of love and kindness, but ignore those in need and act in meanspirited ways. I complain that no one listens to me, but I am deaf to those around me. I make mistakes, but refuse to ask for forgiveness. My words don't match my actions, and I am unfaithful to myself and others.

Ponder: Do I practice what I preach? Do I put myself on a pedestal? Am I willing to give a helping hand to those struggling in life? Can I ask God for the courage to be human?

Prayer: God, help me to keep climbing the mountain of life. Show me the path of honesty and truth.

Practice: Today I will fast from hypocrisy; I will pray for honesty and truth; I will practice what I preach.

Wednesday, the Second Week of Lent
Jeremiah 18:18-20; Matthew 20:17-28

Reflection: I often fantasize about being a "great" person, a saint, someone famous, someone people look up to. The chances of my being great, however, lie in doing my best in the life I have been called to. If I nurture my family and serve the needy where I can; if I do my job with energy and efficiency; if I take care of my physical, spiritual, mental, and emotional well-being; if I do my best in school; if I treat others with respect and dignity—I am doing the work God asks of me. I accept that true greatness comes from being who I am in the light of God's unconditional love.

Ponder: Have I ever plotted against someone? Do I seek revenge against others? Do I think of myself as superior to others? Am I willing to serve others in need? Am I a humble servant?

Prayer: God, help me to keep climbing the mountain of life. Show me the path of self-acceptance.

Practice: Today I will fast from envy of others; I will pray for self-acceptance; I will affirm the dignity of others with a positive word.

Thursday, the Second Week of Lent
Jeremiah 17:5-10; Luke 16:19-31

Reflection: I am insensitive to others when I gossip and talk about them behind their backs. I am selfish when I don't help the poor and homeless in my community. I am indifferent to social problems when I don't take a stand against racism, prejudice, and discrimination. I am irresponsible when I refuse to exercise my right to vote. I ask God for the courage to act out of justice instead of insensitivity, selfishness, indifference, and irresponsibility. God will show me simple ways to change my attitudes and be a positive influence in my community.

Ponder: Do I share only my excess with the needy and poor? Is this true charity? What causes me to be a selfish person? When have I felt poor and in need? How do I improve the quality of life in my community?

Prayer: God, help me to keep climbing the mountain of life. Show me the path of justice.

Practice: Today I will fast from selfishness; I will pray for justice; I will volunteer to participate in a community improvement project.

Friday, the Second Week of Lent
Genesis 37:3-4,12-13,17-28; Matthew 21:33-43,45-46

Reflection: I have often felt insecure and have hurt others because I think they are ganging up on me or plotting against me. Because of my own painful experiences, I try to find ways to make other people's lives uncomfortable or even miserable. I need a change of attitude. I need to cultivate peace in my heart and not give in to violence of thoughts, words, and actions.

Ponder: Do I feel jealous of any of the people in my life?

Does my love ever turn to hate? Do I go along with the crowd in a plot against someone else? Do I gang up on others? Do I respect God and my neighbor?

Prayer: God, help me to keep climbing the mountain of life. Show me the path of peace.

Practice: Today I will fast from violence; I will pray for peace; I will make peace with someone I fear.

Saturday, the Second Week of Lent
Micah 7:14-15,18-20; Luke 15:1-3,11-32

Reflection: Forgiveness is not always easy for me. If others admit that they have hurt me and show me they intend not to repeat the offense, I find it fairly easy to forgive them. There are people, however, who have violated my boundaries and who cannot acknowledge that fact. I must find the willingness to forgive these people if I am to imitate God's mercy.

Ponder: Have I squandered any of the gifts God has given me? Is it possible for me to admit the mistakes I make? Do I tend to turn to God only when I am in dire need? Do I celebrate when others turn to God? Do I experience God's forgiveness in my life? Do I take advantage of the sacrament of reconciliation?

Prayer: God, help me to keep climbing the mountain of life. Show me the path of forgiveness.

Practice: Today I will fast from blame; I will pray for forgiveness; I will let go of a grudge I have been holding.

The Third Week of Lent

Cycle A
Spiritual Thirst for Justice and Love

"The Samaritan woman said to him, 'You are a Jew. How can you ask me, a Samaritan and a woman, for a drink?'" (John 4:9).

Thus far we have journeyed with the Lord into the desert and to the top of the Mountain of Transfiguration. Now we are with him at the site of Jacob's well, tired from our journey. With Jesus we long for a drink of water to refresh our spirit and renew our strength. Water is such a precious gift from God. It is symbolic of God's love, grace, kindness, and mercy. It is a sign of life. Water also cleanses and purifies. What would life be without the gift of water?

With Jesus we have the privilege of meeting a Samaritan and a woman. (Recall that Jews have nothing to do with Samaritans.) Jesus looks beyond the prejudice and hostility between Jews and Samaritans, however, and invites this woman into a relationship of trust and love. Can we do the same thing? How open are we to meeting people we have nothing to do with? How willing are we to confront our own prejudices about people? How committed are we to the cause of racial equality and justice for the oppressed and poor?

This week we reflect on our relationship with God and our neighbors, especially those we have nothing to do with. We drink the water that Jesus offers us each day: the water of love, understanding, compassion, and justice. This is the water that will refresh and renew the face of the earth. This is the water that will cleanse and purify all that separates and divides us from one another. It doesn't matter who we are or what backgrounds we come from. What matters is that Jesus comes to us and asks each of us for a drink. What kind of water do we want to give the Lord?

Third Sunday of Lent—Cycle A
Exodus 17:3-7; Romans 5:1-2,5-8; John 4:5-42

Reflection: At this point in my journey I sit at my own well and examine the water I drink. Perhaps I drink the contaminated water of ethnic cleansing, hatred, resentment, racism, and prejudice. Perhaps my well is dry and I need to look for a new place to draw water. The real challenge is to ask for a drink of water from an individual or a group of people I have deliberately ignored and alienated. Can I imagine Jesus' thirst for a world in which people regard one another as sisters and brothers, where people do their best to ensure equality and justice for everyone regardless of race, nationality, ethnic origin, belief, and way of life? Do I, likewise, have a thirst for true justice and love for everyone in my local and global community?

Ponder: What is the well I drink from? Do I need to change the water I drink? Do I need to change the water I give to others? Does the fountain within me pour out love? Do I believe that God will refresh me when I ask?

Prayer: God, lead me to the well of your loving kindness. Let me drink the water of justice.

Practice: This week I will fast from prejudice and hatred; I will pray for equality among all people; I will give more time to teaching our children and youth to love and respect others.

Cycle B
Turning Things Upside Down

"In the temple precincts he came upon people engaged in selling oxen, sheep and doves, and others seated changing coins. He made a [kind of] whip of cords and drove them all out of the temple area, sheep and oxen alike, and knocked over the money-changers' tables, spilling their coins" (John 2:14-15).

The Temple was a sacred place for the Jewish people. It was the place where they met their God in prayer and worship. The Temple was also the heart of the Jewish community because it was the symbol of God's covenant of love. How could anyone misinterpret the rich symbolism of the Temple and its importance in Jewish life? What happens to people when they fail to remember what is essential and important in life?

Jesus drives everyone out of the Temple precincts, including the animals, because he wants the people to respect their sacred places. Jesus knows how critical it is to minimize a marketplace mentality if we are to connect with God.

But we live in a predominantly capitalistic and materialistic world. It takes great effort on our part to separate ourselves from the marketplace mentality of competition, personal achievement, and success at any cost. We are preoccupied with the daily problems of life, work, relationships, personal interest, and finances. Our anxiety and stress are enough to drown out existence itself.

Fortunately, we have a spiritual temple within ourselves where we can encounter God: the sanctuary of our hearts. It is important for us to keep this temple clean and pure, full of love and peace. This week we spend time in our spiritual temple, that inner place where the Lord dwells, where we enter into communion with the God who loved us first. We make the effort to connect with God on a deeper level. We become aware of the many distractions that keep us from being in communion with God. We cleanse our hearts of all the unnecessary baggage that replaces our relationship with the Lord.

If we lose our connection with God, we lose the promise of new life. We need to spend some time rebuilding the inner sanctuary of our hearts, finding a place within to connect with the God of peace and love.

Third Sunday of Lent—Cycle B
Exodus 20:1-17; 1 Corinthians 1:22-25; John 2:13-25

Reflection: If I lose my connection with God, I lose the promise of new life. If I want to be more aware of my need for God, I must find a place—a quiet place—where God and I can be alone. There, in that place, I can cultivate and nurture my spirituality so that I will not be overwhelmed by the glitter and glamour of the secular world. I cannot give in to the temptation to live life without God. In this rapidly changing world, I want to slow the pace and get my priorities in order. This means turning my life upside down and getting rid of anything that keeps me from being at peace within myself, with my God, and with others.

Ponder: Do God's commandments seem practical to me? Do I ever fail to carry them out? Which commandment is the hardest for me to follow? Would Jesus trust me? Do I include God in my everyday life? Does my inner sanctuary need to be cleansed?

Prayer: God, lead me to the well of your loving kindness. Let me drink the water of serenity.

Practice: This week I will fast from excessive competition with others; I will pray for humility in moments of temptation; I will share the peace I find in God by choosing peaceful words when I speak.

Cycle C
For Better or for Worse

"At that time some were present who told Jesus about the Galileans whose blood Pilate had mixed with their sacrifices. He said in reply: 'Do you think that these Galileans were the greatest sinners in Galilee just because they suffered this? By no means! But I tell you, you will all come to the same end unless you reform'" (Luke 13:1-3).

What we do in light of who we are has a tremendous impact in the world. In essence, if we claim to be children of God then it is expected that we think and act in the light of God's loving mercy and kindness. Yet, our daily routine is often done without much awareness of the fact that God is working in and through us. We simply wake up in the morning and go about business as usual. As children of God, however, we must have the intention to be like God in the world: slow to anger, rich in kindness, and full of love.

This week we listen to the voice of God, we seize the opportunities to do good for others, and we make a fundamental change in the way we approach life. We no longer stand in the background and pretend that everything is all right in the world. We are no longer mere human spectators watching the world fall apart right before our eyes. We no longer run and hide from the harsh realities of prejudice, discrimination, and indifference.

Instead, we reflect upon the quality of our relationship with God and with others. We awake with a determination to live life in the light of love, for to refuse to love is to accept doom. We turn away from the old feelings of hatred, resentment, anger, and revenge, and look for the goodness in others. We embrace others out of a deep sense of spiritual connectedness. We broadened our narrow vision of life to welcome the stranger into our lives. We explore ways in which people from every background and way of life can come together to learn about one another and to grow in mutual respect and understanding.

No matter how difficult life might be at times, we must never lose sight of the fact that we are connected, one to the other, and that together we journey toward the kingdom of God. Unless we reform and do our best to love one another we will all come to the "same end." We have options. What we ultimately decide can be for the better or for the worse!

Third Sunday of Lent—Cycle C
Exodus 3:1-8,13-15; 1 Corinthians 10:1-6,10-12; Luke 13:19

Reflection: I am at another crossroad in life and the world community needs to know that there is a better way to live in the midst of diversity. I don't have to violate others; I don't have to yield to violence; I don't have to harbor thoughts and feelings of hatred toward others. God gives me the time I need to bring about change—and that change must begin with me. I must be willing to reform the way I have approached life and people. I must not look at people as my enemies but rather as true icons of God.

Ponder: Am I afraid to look at God? Am I afraid to have God look at me? Do I grumble about my lot in life? What do I need to reform? Do I imitate God's loving mercy and kindness in my dealings with others? Do I ever refuse to love? Do I ever refuse to be loved?

Prayer: God, lead me to the well of your loving kindness. Let me drink the water of transformation.

Practice: This week I will fast from giving in to feelings of resentment and revenge; I will pray for the willingness to accept the diversity of God's people around me; I will treat others with loving kindness.

Monday, the Third Week of Lent
2 Kings 5:1-15; Luke 4:24-30

Reflection: The words and suggestions of someone who is not emotionally close to me are often easier for me to listen to and follow than those of someone I care about deeply. It may be a fear of intimacy that blocks my willingness to listen. It may be that I am slightly contemptuous of someone I know well. It may be a fear of being controlled. It may be that I have judged my friends and family and have decided their wisdom and experiences are limited.

Ponder: Do I recognize my need for healing? Am I waiting for a miracle to cure me of spiritual, mental, physical, or emotional pain? Am I willing to ask for help with this pain? What is my attitude toward people living with HIV/AIDS?

Prayer: God, lead me to the well of your loving kindness. Let me drink the water of loving patience.

Practice: Today I will fast from contempt; I will pray for the patience to listen; I will hear without judging what others say.

Tuesday, the Third Week of Lent
Daniel 3:25,34-43; Matthew 18:21-35

Reflection: Forgiving someone who has hurt me; forgiving someone who constantly gets on my nerves; forgiving someone who violates my physical, mental, spiritual, or emotional boundaries in petty or invasive ways: this is critical to my spiritual growth. Forgiveness belongs to God and God shares this gift with me. When I control God's forgiveness and refuse to let it go, I hold it back out of fear of being hurt, ignored, and alienated. Remembering that God constantly forgives me and wants me to share this gift with others helps me offer the gift of forgiveness even when it's difficult.

Ponder: Do I treat all people with equal respect? Do I expect mercy from God? Am I patient with other people's weaknesses? What do I need God to deliver me from? Do I forgive and forget?

Prayer: God, lead me to the well of your loving kindness. Let me drink the water of forgiveness.

Practice: Today I will fast from holding a grudge against my neighbor; I will pray for the strength to forgive someone who has hurt me; I will be kind to those who hurt me.

Wednesday, the Third Week of Lent
Deuteronomy 4:1,5-9; Matthew 5:17-19

Reflection: When my words and actions reflect a peaceful, loving heart, and when I put my life and will into God's merciful care, I am a living example of what it means to be in the kingdom of God. God's kingdom surrounds me and is in me. I need to open my eyes and ears and heart to the beauty of that kingdom. It doesn't take much for me to slip into old ways of pessimism, negativity, sarcasm, and rebellion. As I discipline myself to walk in God's ways, however, I can just as easily slip out of those old habits into the joy of participating in God's kingdom.

Ponder: How much wisdom do I show in the way I lead my life? Is there anyone who teaches me the way to the kingdom of God? Do I believe that holiness is within my reach? Do I believe that God will show me the path of holiness if I ask?

Prayer: God, lead me to the well of your loving kindness. Let me drink the water of the peace of your kingdom.

Practice: Today I will fast from negativity; I will pray for joy; I will look for God's kingdom in the beauty of creation.

Thursday, the Third Week of Lent
Jeremiah 7:23-28; Luke 11:14-23

Reflection: I can disagree with someone without being disagreeable. I do not have to force people to agree with my way of life or my opinions. Although it is important for me to speak out against injustice, bigotry, abuse, and other evils, it is possible to do so in a peaceful way and in a way that supports the dignity of the people with whom I am interacting. I need to keep in mind that in order to promote change, I must work with people as a messenger of God. Forced solutions, put-downs, violence of speech and behavior, power struggles, chaos, and dissension are not God's ways of interacting.

Ponder: Am I with God or against God? Where is there dissension in my life? Have I turned my back on anyone? Do I ever turn my back on God? Are there demons in me—such as prejudice, hatred, fear, addictions, violence, rage—that I need to ask the Lord to cast out?

Prayer: God, lead me to the well of your loving kindness. Let me drink the water of unity.

Practice: Today I will fast from dissension; I will pray for unity; I will listen with respect to the opinions of my sisters and brothers.

Friday, the Third Week of Lent
Hosea 14:2-10; Mark 12:28-34

Reflection: The greatest challenge in my life is loving myself. I wake up some days and feel ugly inside; I don't feel I am good enough or worthy enough to be loved. Sometimes I am afraid to let others love me for fear that I might have to love them in return. I don't always feel comfortable with love because it makes me vulnerable. I need to remind myself that love is one of God's beautiful gifts, and as I learn to appreciate and love myself, I will begin to trust God and God's love for me. I will then be able to reach out and love others.

Ponder: How do my words and actions reflect the commandment to love? Do I ever allow the Spirit of love to change me? Do I love myself? Who is the neighbor I find difficult to love? Why am I afraid to love?

Prayer: God, lead me to the well of your loving kindness. Let me drink the water of love.

Practice: Today I will fast from self-hatred; I will pray for love; I will say "I love you" to myself, to someone close to me, and to God.

Saturday, the Third Week of Lent
Hosea 6:1-6; Luke 18:9-14

Reflection: I waste time comparing myself to others and, even if I come out on top, I still must face the truth that I am a weak and frail person like everyone else. It is so hard for me to accept this truth about myself. Maybe this is why I put people down, misjudge character, and act superior to others. I need to accept that every person is as special as I am and that we all have the potential to be like Jesus: full of love, peace, and compassion.

Ponder: How do I pray? Do I spend my days comparing myself to others? Can I accept myself as I am and ask God to be merciful to me? Am I self-righteous? Do I insist on having my own way? Do I love as best I can? Do I pray for a humble and contrite heart?

Prayer: God, lead me to the well of your loving kindness. Let me drink the water of humility.

Practice: Today I will fast from putting people down; I will pray for humility; I will find something good to say about others.

The Fourth Week of Lent

Cycle A
To See or Not to See

"'I know this much: I was blind before; now I can see'" (John 9:25).

Thus far we have been with the Lord in the desert, on the mountain, and at the well. In each of these moments we were invited to enter into a totally new relationship with Jesus, opening up possibilities for us to become new persons in light of God's grace, mercy, and love.

This week we come face-to-face with the man born blind. With Jesus, we stop and dialogue with this man, this beggar, this marginal person. Along with Jesus, we watch people walking by, ignoring this man, denying the fact that he is a child of God who needs acceptance and love. There is no greater blindness than this kind of moral and spiritual blindness: the inability to see the people around us as living icons of the God of love.

Perhaps the real sin of today's world is moral blindness: our failure to love the people we see and encounter each day. We do not work hard enough to see God's image in others. This might explain why there is an increase in abuse and violence toward the weak, greater insensitivity toward the poor, increasing disrespect for life, and growing hostility toward people of different ethnic, cultural, and racial backgrounds.

The man born blind ultimately wants to see Jesus and when he finally realizes that he has actually seen the Lord, he bows down to worship in faith and love. The story pricks our conscience and helps us reexamine our attitude toward others in the light of our relationship with Jesus. One of our greatest blessings is to be able to sit at the eucharistic table and, with the eyes of faith, see Jesus under the appearance of bread and wine. As we share the Eucharist, our eyes are opened to this miracle of love, peace, and forgiveness, and we are transformed into a new reality for the sake of building God's kingdom on earth. As people of faith, we cannot walk around with inner blindfolds, but must be about God's work of love, peace, and compassion in the world.

Fourth Sunday of Lent—Cycle A
1 Samuel 16:1,6-7,10-13; Ephesians 5:8-14; John 9:1-41

Reflection: At this point in my Lenten journey I need to get in touch with my own inner blindness. What keeps me from seeing God in others? What keeps me from seeing the needs of my neighbors? Why do I allow myself to be blinded by anger, hate, jealousy, prejudice, resentment, and revenge? Why am I afraid to love and be loved in return? In the light of Jesus I need to recognize my strengths and weaknesses. I need to believe that I am an immensely good person and that I have what I need to live in peace and harmony with everyone.

Ponder: Where am I blind? Can I ask Jesus to heal my blindness? What makes me blind to self-love? Do I judge people by their appearance? Do I take the time to look into people's hearts? Do I know my own heart? Do I discern what I *need* to see from what I *want* to see?

Prayer: God, heal my blindness. Open my eyes to see your image in others.

Practice: This week I will fast from self-hatred; I will pray for openness to others; I will give more to Operation Rice Bowl to help the poor and marginalized around the world.

Cycle B
Costly Love

"'God loved the world so much, he gave us his only Son, / that all who believe in him might have eternal life'" (John 3:16).

Just imagine letting go of the most precious possession in life. No one asks that this be done and no one demands that this be done under penalty of death. This unsolicited and generous act of love is God's way of dealing with a world that doesn't always want to love.

This week we reflect upon the great sacrifice of love that God made for humankind. We don't often think about the way in which God loves us. God did not send us an inanimate object as a sign of love. God did not rain down money from heaven to show us love. God did not propose a list of conditions for us to consider before demonstrating such great love. Rather, God sent us a living person, a beloved Son, filled with enduring love, to save the world. We know and experience this love through faith in Jesus.

As we reflect upon God's love for us, we consider the ways in which we share and don't share the gift of God's love. Do we hold back love when we meet someone who has a different color complexion, speaks a different language, comes from a different socioeconomic background, or lives a different lifestyle? Do we condemn people out of fear and ignorance? Or do we respond to the Spirit of God by offering the gift that was given to us through God's only Son, the costly gift of love?

We must remember that we participate in God's love and are called to take the risk of loving others. When we acknowledge our failure to love and seek God's forgiveness, we recommit ourselves to the task of consciously sharing the gift of God's love in every human situation. When we use the standard of

God's costly love as a point of reference, the events of our lives take on an entirely new meaning and our actions have a greater impact on the whole spectrum of life.

Fourth Sunday of Lent—Cycle B
2 Chronicles 36:14-17,19-23; Ephesians 2:4-10; John 3:14-21

Reflection: Perhaps my greatest challenge in life is learning how to release into the world the passionate love of God which is deep within my own heart. God took a great risk in giving this world—my world—a Savior. At the risk of being humiliated, rejected, and despised by many, God chose to love unconditionally. I can see that love is not about being in control; it is not about power and manipulation. True love makes me powerless and vulnerable and this is why I find it so difficult to love. I just don't want to be hurt in the process; I don't want to die. When I become afraid and doubt my capacity to love, I only need to remember the promise that God made: whoever believes in him will not die, but will have eternal life (John 3:15).

Ponder: Have there been messengers of God in my life? Do I scoff at God's messengers? How has God shown mercy to me? How has God's kindness been manifested to me? Do I show mercy and kindness to myself and others? How do I love? Generously? wholeheartedly? selfishly? manipulatively? vulnerably?

Prayer: God, heal my blindness. Open my eyes to see your gifts of love.

Practice: This week I will fast from doubting my capacity to love; I will pray for forgiveness for resisting love; I will risk being vulnerable by loving others.

Cycle C
Hospitality and Forgiveness

"The tax collectors and the sinners were all gathering around Jesus to hear him, at which the Pharisees and the scribes murmured, 'This man welcomes sinners and eats with them'" (Luke 15:1-3).

Jesus goes out of his way to associate with known sinners. He deliberately chooses to be with them and eat with them. Sinners are his friends. What is so terrible about this extraordinary display of hospitality, compassion, and forgiveness? Aren't known sinners human beings? Aren't they children of God? Don't known sinners deserve the same respect as everyone else in the community? Aren't we all sinners?

Perhaps the Pharisees and the scribes who murmur about Jesus' attitude and behavior toward sinners tend to forget that they, too, are sinners in need of God's mercy and forgiveness. On a much larger scale, they do not recognize the fact that they are filled with arrogance and pride. Somehow the Pharisees and the scribes think they are better than everyone else.

The person of Jesus stands in sharp contrast to the Pharisees and the scribes. With Jesus there is no rush to judgment, no hesitation to welcome another brother or sister, no resistance to share love with a stranger, no fear of being seen in public with "certain people," no condemnation. Jesus reveals the loving mercy and kindness of God to everyone he encounters. Jesus' approach to others is gentle and peaceful.

Once we experience the loving mercy and forgiveness of God, we will reach out to others with the same loving mercy and forgiveness. We will offer our sisters and brothers the opportunity to know Jesus through our own love. The doorway to healing begins with an attitude of hospitality and a true desire to practice the art of forgiveness with those we find most difficult to work with, to live with, and to worship with. We must be open to the Spirit of God because we never know who has been invited to dinner.

The sin of our times is the failure to recognize our need for a Savior. We walk through life as if we can save ourselves from self-destruction. We must come to our senses before it is too late; we must realize that we need Jesus and his love, mercy, compassion, and forgiveness if we are to have inner peace. We cannot give these gifts to ourselves. Only someone greater than ourselves can offer us what we truly need in this life. Jesus walks into our world and invites us to taste and see the goodness of the Lord. There are no strings attached, no pre-conditions. There is unconditional love and acceptance of our broken humanity.

Fourth Sunday of Lent—Cycle C
Joshua 5:9,10-12; 2 Corinthians 5:17-21; Luke 15:1-3,11-32

Reflection: During this season I am challenged to become more aware of how Jesus invites me to be with him and to dine with him. First, I acknowledge the fact that I am a sinner, that I am in need of inner healing and peace. I must believe in the sanctuary of my heart that I can be and am forgiven by a gracious God. The tax collectors and the sinners knew that Jesus was not out to destroy them. They had come to know Jesus as a friend and companion on their journey in life.

Ponder: Are there certain people I would not share a meal with because they are: from a different culture, embrace a different faith tradition, have an opinion about abortion that doesn't agree with mine, have alcohol or drug addictions? Do I judge others? What habits do I have that go against God's ways? Do I believe God will show me the way to change? Do I practice forgiveness in my life on a daily basis?

Prayer: God, heal my blindness. Open my eyes to see your presence in the people I meet.

Practice: This week I will fast from judgment; I will pray for a spirit of hospitality and forgiveness; I will invite someone to share a snack or simple meal with me.

Monday, the Fourth Week of Lent
Isaiah 65:17-21; John 4:43-54

Reflection: I ask God for help, but it is difficult for me to leave matters in God's loving hands. I continue to worry and fret; my mind circles constantly around the same problem until I am anxious and tired. I need to remember that I worry because I feel powerless, but by turning the problem over to God, I surrender my need to feel powerful or in control. I gently remind myself to trust that God will answer me in God's time and in the way that is best for me.

Ponder: Can I imagine a new, peaceful earth? Am I waiting for God to give me a sign about the changes I need to make in my life? Do I look for God's wonder in everyday happenings? Do I trust that God will answer my cries for help? What will it take to make me a believer in God's healing, loving kindness, and mercy?

Prayer: God, heal my blindness. Open my eyes to see your loving kindness.

Practice: Today I will fast from putting myself down; I will pray for trust in my own goodness; I will keep my thoughts in the present moment instead of worrying.

Tuesday, the Fourth Week of Lent
Ezekiel 47:1-9,12; John 5:1-3,5-16

Reflection: I assume that if no one shows love for me, I am not lovable. I don't even love myself. Yet, because God created me in love, I am lovable. Doing loving things for myself is one way to learn to love myself: buying a flower, taking a walk, sitting in the sun, going for a hike, gathering with friends, saying *I love you* to myself, believing others when they tell me "I love you." While I am learning to love myself, I will also be learning how to love others and God.

Ponder: Do I wait for others to make me happy? Do I ever deliberately choose to be happy? Do I love myself? Would I say "Yes" if Jesus asked me if I wanted to be healed? Is there a payoff for me *not* to be healed? Am I willing to give up my shortcomings in order to be healed?

Prayer: God, heal my blindness. Open my eyes to see your love for me.

Practice: Today I will fast from false expectations; I will pray for self-love; I will do one loving thing for myself, one for a neighbor, one for God.

Wednesday, the Fourth Week of Lent
Isaiah 49:8-15; John 5:17-30

Reflection: When a problem arises, I think I have to provide the solution. I am learning, however, that only God has all the answers. By placing my life and will into God's hands, I surrender the problem to God. Solutions will gradually come to me once I surrender the problem in quiet prayer, in nature, or in talking to trusted friends. I need to be open to God's solutions in people I meet, in the world around me, and in the deepest part of my being.

Ponder: Do I ask for help when life's problems are difficult, or do I tend to isolate? Is it hard for me to accept that I cannot do anything alone? Do I seek God's will in everything I do? Do I remember to check in with God when times are hard? Do I remember to check in with God when times are good? Do I refuse help when people offer it to me?

Prayer: God, heal my blindness. Open my eyes to see your truth and wisdom.

Practice: Today I will fast from thinking that I am better than the next person; I will pray for the will power to seek spiritual guidance; I will thank a friend who supports me.

Thursday, the Fourth Week of Lent
Exodus 32:7-14; John 5:31-47

Reflection: I feel good about myself when someone praises me, but I am not always generous with praise for others. I feel good about myself when others appreciate my kindness, but I am not always appreciative of the little things others do for me. I feel good about myself when someone I love hugs me and tells me I am loved, but I am not always free with my expressions of love. Looking for opportunities to praise and appreciate others helps me to be a more mindful and loving person, aware of the needs of others.

Ponder: When does my love blaze as bright as my anger? Do I have the love of God in my heart? What will it take for me to accept God's love? Am I grateful to God for all that I have in life?

Prayer: God, heal my blindness. Open my eyes to see your goodness and generosity.

Practice: Today I will fast from taking people for granted; I will pray for gratitude; I will say "please" and "thank you" when kindness is offered to me.

Friday, the Fourth Week of Lent
Wisdom 2:1,12-22; John 7:1-2,10,25-30

Reflection: I have faults and I have strengths: impatient one minute, patient the next; rude one minute, kind the next; crying one minute, laughing the next; resentful one minute, forgiving the next; indifferent one minute, loving the next. I am human, and I am made in God's image and likeness. As I begin to accept the mixture that I am, I learn to maintain an even balance in my thoughts, emotions, and actions.

Ponder: Do I know myself? Do I know God? Do I believe God knows me? What wickedness blinds me? Fear? shame? arrogance? self-righteousness? an addiction? What am I hiding from God and others?

Prayer: God, heal my blindness. Open my eyes to see your patience and mercy.

Practice: Today I will fast from inconsistent behavior; I will pray for inner balance; I will think before I act.

Saturday, the Fourth Week of Lent
Jeremiah 11:18-20; John 7:40-53

Reflection: Even when I feel in my heart that I am doing God's will, my mind can convince me that I am foolish to trust this feeling. Because instinct is hard to put into words and intuition is not provable with facts, my mind will overrule my heart by presenting me with fearful memories, facts, and evidence so that I am afraid to be vulnerable again. God's call, however, is to follow the way of love, kindness, compassion, and mercy without fear for myself.

Ponder: Is my faith dependent on facts alone? Do I lose my capacity for loving kindness and mercy by following rules and doctrines too rigidly? When God searches my mind and heart, what is there to find? Do I trust God, the Mystery?

Prayer: God, heal my blindness. Open my eyes to see your gentle spirit.

Practice: Today I will fast from thinking about too many things; I will pray for serenity; I will listen more and speak less.

The Fifth Week of Lent

Cycle A
The Spirit of Life Within Us

"The sisters sent word to Jesus to inform him, 'Lord, the one you love is sick.' Upon hearing this, Jesus said: / 'This sickness is not to end in death; / rather it is for God's glory, / that through it the Son of God may be glorified'"(John 11:3-4).

Sickness and suffering are part of the human condition. We see sickness and suffering in our families, in our communities, and around the world. Sometimes the sickness and suffering we experience and hear about distract us from the essence of humanity: the Spirit of God's life within us.

This week we enter into one of the most beautiful and loving stories in all of Scripture. We walk into the home of Mary and Martha who, with their Jewish friends, are weeping over the death of Lazarus. Jesus is filled with emotion and love for his friend and cries with them. Jesus, the Compassion of God, loves so deeply. If only we can remember this when we are sick, in pain, and suffering.

Sickness and suffering are personal. We feel broken inside. We struggle to understand the meaning and purpose of the pain and, at times, actually wrestle with our fear of death. The story of Jesus raising Lazarus from the dead is a foretaste of the new life Jesus offers those who sincerely believe that he is the resurrection and the life. No matter what we suffer in this life, we must remember what our faith teaches us: suffering is not the end of life but the beginning of a spiritual awakening of the transforming power of God's life and love within us.

Do we believe that Jesus is with us in our brokenness and pain? Do we believe that Jesus walks with us in our suffering? Do we believe that Jesus loves us unconditionally and gives us the strength and peace we need to live each day in hope?

This week we embrace and accept the pain and suffering in our lives. Jesus does not deny the fact that Lazarus is dead. Instead, he confronts death and teaches us how to accept our hurts and suffering. He shows us how to accept death graciously by focusing on the gospel of life.

Fifth Sunday of Lent—Cycle A
Ezekiel 37:12-14; Romans 8:8-11; John 11:1-45

Reflection: Every day Jesus comes to me and offers me the possibility of living a new life. I can accept that invitation only when I live with a new attitude: love. Without love, I die. Without hope, I have no meaningful future. Without faith in Jesus, I have no foundation in life. Jesus comes to me and offers me faith, hope, love, and eternal life. The Spirit of God's life is within me and nothing, not even sickness and death, can separate me from God's life and love.

Ponder: Am I asleep or awake to God? Have I ever wept for a dead friend or family member? What do I feel like when I am troubled in spirit? What do I do with my pain and suffering? To whom do I turn when I am afraid to die?

Prayer: God, show me the Spirit of your life within me so that I may transform my suffering into faith.

Practice: This week I will fast from complaining about my hurts and pains; I will pray for inner healing; I will visit someone who is hospitalized or is in a nursing home.

"'I solemnly assure you, / unless the grain of wheat falls to the earth and dies, / it remains just a grain of wheat. / But if it dies, / it produces much fruit'" (John 12:24).

Jesus uses the image of a grain of wheat to describe the process of personal conversion and transformation. The use of this pastoral image—the grain of wheat falling to the earth—reminds us of another image used to describe the creation of man and woman. In the Book of Genesis we read about how God created man and woman from the clay of the earth and breathed new life into them. The earth which was made holy by God is connected to the creation and development of humankind.

This week we reflect on the precious gift of life given to us by God. This gift is holy and finds its beginning and end with God. We also reflect on the gift of the earth and how we can advocate for environmental or ecological justice. We forget that our life and the earth are connected and that our life is endangered when we do not take care of our environment.

The grain of wheat that falls to the earth and dies is symbolic of one of the necessary rituals of life that we must embody if we are to grow and mature. This ritual is not limited to the physical dimension of human existence, but includes the emotional, mental, and spiritual dimensions as well. If we don't allow the grain of love to fall into the soil of our hearts, we will not be able to feel the love of another person. If we don't allow the grain of peace to be implanted in the soil of our minds, we will not be able to create a vision of peace for the world. If we don't allow the grain of compassion to be one with the soil of our human spirit, we will not be able to walk in solidarity with the poor and suffering.

All of this presupposes a willingness on our part to reaffirm the precious gift of life through the ritual of personal conversion. Each day we have an opportunity to renew the heart, mind, spirit, and body through a discipline of prayer, self-examination, spiritual reading, and re-creation with others. This discipline will produce much fruit for life. There will be more peace in the world, more concern for the well-being of our sisters and brothers, a greater sense of compassion for the poor and needy, and more respect for the human race.

The ritual of dying and rising to new life begins when we can say no to the distractions of life and concentrate on God's life within us. This also requires dying to the old rituals of wasting time on foolishness, watching too much television, eating junk food, and spending too much money on things we don't need.

Fifth Sunday of Lent—Cycle B
Jeremiah 31:31-34; Hebrews 5:7-9; John 12:20-33

Reflection: I can produce much fruit if I learn how to live with a deeper and more profound appreciation for life and the environment. In the beginning God created me—and all creation—from the earth, which was a place of peace. I will return to this place one day only to bear the fruit of eternal life in God's kingdom. Unless I am willing to fall to the earth and die, I shall remain a mere grain of wheat.

Ponder: Is obedience something that comes easily to me? Do I enjoy obeying God? Do I believe that new life will evolve for me when I let go of old patterns of behavior? Does my present manner of living produce much fruit for the Lord? Do I serve my neighbors and God to the best of my ability? Do I cling to life here on earth? Am I afraid to die?

Prayer: God, show me the Spirit of your life within me so that I may produce the fruits of love, peace, and compassion.

Practice: This week I will fast from being caught up in and distracted by petty things; I will pray for a deeper reverence for life; I will pick up any litter I see as I move about my community.

Cycle C
Empowering with Love

"The scribes and the Pharisees led a woman forward who had been caught in adultery. They made her stand there in front of everyone" (John 8:3).

Some people take great delight in meddling in the personal affairs of others. Some people cannot wait to hear a rumor or make up a meanspirited story about others. Some people enjoy making public the sins and faults of others, especially those who are considered second-class citizens and human pawns. We all know people who have been harshly treated because of their way of life.

Some prominent men, scribes and Pharisees, decide to abuse a woman who has already experienced emotional, mental, spiritual, and physical trauma. They lead her into the public forum and expose her sin of adultery. Her public humiliation and shame is surely unbearable.

The woman caught in adultery represents all those who have been disempowered by the constant abuse of others. This week we are called to look deep within our hearts to ask some basic questions: Do we want others to know about our dark secrets and sins? How would it feel to trade places with the woman caught in adultery? How do we treat people of diverse backgrounds? How do we treat women? In what ways do we abuse the people around us?

We live in a multimedia environment in which the sins and faults of others are quickly exposed in newspapers, magazines, journals, and television. There seems to be a sick fascination with prying open the private areas of people's lives to bring them dishonor and shame. Jesus exposes the power of God's love by not giving in to the games of the scribes and the Pharisees. Jesus exposes not the sin of the woman but rather her basic goodness; he guides her into a deeper understanding of self without condemnation and judgment. Jesus leaves the woman's integrity intact and does not manipulate her mind, heart, and spirit.

We can all think of moments when we were not faithful to God, ourselves, and others. These shameful memories from the past hold us captive, and we keep hoping for someone to liberate us from this mental and emotional bondage. The great lesson we learn from the story of the woman caught in adultery is that we empower free people by loving them, not by putting them down. The one thing we need to do in public is love one another as God loves us. This will have a tremendous impact on the world and will help liberate people from their fears, guilt, and shame.

At the end of the story Jesus tells the woman to go in peace and to avoid this sin. Jesus tells us the same thing: be at peace and simply love one another.

Fifth Sunday of Lent—Cycle C
Isaiah 43:16-21; Philippians 3:8-14; John 8:1-11

Reflection: I do not have the right to set up anyone for judgment and condemnation. No justice is achieved when people expose the secrets and sins of others. No good comes out of such vicious schemes. With Jesus as my model, I will work to uphold the dignity of others instead of plotting to humiliate them.

Ponder: Have I ever been disempowered? Have I ever disempowered another? Have I ever been publicly shamed? Have I ever shamed anyone in public? Do I meddle in the lives of others? Do I appreciate others meddling in my life? Do I treat others with justice and loving kindness? Do I believe that God's love empowers me? Am I willing to use my love to empower others?

Prayer: God, show me the Spirit of your life within me so that I may empower others by loving them unconditionally.

Practice: This week I will fast from intentionally hurting others; I will pray for a deeper understanding of myself and others; I will lovingly support my family and neighbors in times of trouble.

Monday, the Fifth Week of Lent
Daniel 13:1-9,15-17,19-30,33-62; John 8:1-11

Reflection: When I am tempted to condemn others for their actions and behaviors, I look at my own life and see that I have done many hurtful and sinful things. I know that I am capable of almost any harmful deed: betrayal, violence, gossip, deceit, rejection, theft, abuse, lying. How can I condemn someone else when I know the harm I have done in the past, the harm I am doing now, and the harm I may do in the future?

Ponder: Do I condemn others for their actions? Have I ever done anything harmful? Do I have the potential for doing more harm? Am I able to avoid the behaviors that have hurt others in the past? Do I call on the Lord in times of temptation and trouble? Do I believe in God's mercy and forgiveness?

Prayer: God, show me the Spirit of your life within me so that I may treat others with compassion.

Practice: Today I will fast from taking part in rude gossip about others; I will pray for compassion and understanding; I will listen to others without judging them.

Tuesday, the Fifth Week of Lent
Numbers 21:4-9; John 8:21-30

Reflection: I keep busy because I define my worth by what I do: I am a parent, I am a wage earner, I am a student, I am a volunteer, I am a good cook, I am an animal lover, I am a minister, I am a pacifist, I am a spouse. In reality, the only definition of worthiness I need is: I am. God has given me life; therefore, I am worthwhile and I am worthy of respect. God created me in love; therefore, I am lovable. My worth and "lovability" have nothing to do with my lifestyle, my job, my race, my social position, my religion, my capacity to perform tasks. My worth and lovability are simply in my being.

Ponder: How do I define my worth as a human person? How do I define the worth of others? Do I believe that being loved is contingent upon my achievements? Do I consider the elderly, persons with disabilities, or those who are critically ill worthy of love and respect?

Prayer: God, show me the Spirit of your life within me so that I may live with dignity.

Practice: Today I will fast from overcrowding my schedule; I will pray for balance in my life; I will sit quietly alone for ten minutes and be with myself.

Wednesday, the Fifth Week of Lent
Daniel 3:14-20,91-92,95; John 8:31-42

Reflection: I am not always honest with myself and the people around me. I cannot always admit when I'm wrong; I cannot always admit when I don't know the answer; I cannot always admit when I'm feeling sad or angry or lonely or tired or fearful; I cannot always admit when I feel alienated from God. There are probably many layers of dishonesty covering up the beautiful truth of my being. As I work to focus the light of honesty on my life, however, I learn to accept myself more easily. I do not feel it necessary to hide the truth of my mental, emotional, physical, and spiritual states. The beautiful truth of my being—that I am loved and that I love—shines forth.

Ponder: In what way and manner do I serve God? How am I a disciple of Jesus? How have I been enslaved by sin? What does it feel like to be a slave to anger? shame? alcohol? fear? another person's emotions? Do I believe Jesus will set me free?

Prayer: God, show me the Spirit of your life within me so that I may live in honesty.

Practice: Today I will fast from dishonesty; I will pray for honesty; I will speak honestly about my thoughts and feelings.

Thursday, the Fifth Week of Lent
Genesis 17:3-9; John 8:51-59

Reflection: There are times when I do not follow through on an agreement with a friend, a coworker, or a family member. Perhaps it is as simple as not keeping an appointment; perhaps it is as thoughtless as forgetting my child's birthday; perhaps it is as devastating as being unfaithful to my spouse. Somehow I need to make amends for breaking my word: an apology, a change in attitude, a change in behavior. I want people to trust me, so I must do my best to be worthy of trust.

Ponder: Has God ever broken a promise to me? Have I ever broken a promise to God? What prompts me to promise God anything? Am I bargaining? Am I trying to control a situation? Do I know God? Do I believe God knows me?

Prayer: God, show me the Spirit of your life within me so that I may live faithfully.

Practice: Today I will fast from breaking my word; I will pray for faithfulness; I will be true to my word.

Friday, the Fifth Week of Lent
Jeremiah 20:10-13; John 10:31-42

Reflection: The shopping I do for an elderly person; the gentle touch I use to bathe my baby; the visit I make to the nursing home; the good meal I make for my family; the smile I give a stranger; the help I give classmates; the fun I have playing with children; the time I spend with a person dying of AIDS; the loving words I use to address others: these are all manifestations of God in me. To connect with people in these simple ways is to bring God to them.

Ponder: Do I connect with others daily or do I tend to isolate? What gestures of love do I show others? Do I generously share God's love with the people I encounter?

Prayer: God, show me the Spirit of your life within me so that I may live in solidarity with others.

Practice: Today I will fast from isolating myself from others; I will pray for a sense of community; I will plan something special with my friends or family.

Saturday, the Fifth Week of Lent
Ezekiel 37:21-28; John 11:45-57

Reflection: A sanctuary is a safe place, a place where I can be myself with no pretenses, where no one threatens me, where I am free to dream in peace, where I connect with God, where I feel love. My home, a church, the woods, a mountain: any of these can be a place of safety and peace and connectedness and love. In this busy world, it is important for me to know my sanctuaries, those places where I find peace and tranquility, for this is how I renew myself physically, emotionally, mentally, and spiritually.

Ponder: Where do I go when I need peace? Where do I go to feel connected to God and others? Do I take the time to seek sanctuary when life gets busy? How do I renew myself?

Prayer: God, show me the Spirit of your life within me that I may live in peace.

Practice: Today I will fast from being a cause of chaos and disunity; I will pray for serenity; I will find a place to pray and reflect.

Holy Week

Cycle A
Compassion: The Fruit of Suffering

"Rather, he emptied himself / and took the form of a slave, / being born in the likeness of men" (Philippians 2:7).

This week we enter into our own passion, pain, and suffering and unite it with the experience of Jesus. No matter what we do to tune out our pain and suffering, we cannot avoid it. Although we have been taught to numb our suffering, to drink it away, to medicate it away, to deny it, to replace it with some other quick fix, this is not the message of the gospel.

Jesus embraces his passion, his suffering. He accepts it because this is God's way of showing the world an extraordinary love. What is the meaning of pain and suffering without love? How can one endure pain and suffering without love? Why does love have to hurt so much? These are questions that arise out of deeply painful moments of life, when we search for answers to the meaning of life, when we feel all alone and afraid, when we struggle out of weakness to love and be faithful to ourselves and others.

Jesus empties himself, giving us a powerful example of self-disclosure. He wants to be the sign of God's love in a world that is not ready to accept love in this way. Perhaps the most difficult love to understand is the love birthed out of human suffering. When we are in pain, we usually don't think about God's love and the truth that we are loved and lovable. We feel so useless and helpless, so weak and powerless. Perhaps this is the point at which we come to understand the meaning of the cross and why God chooses this way to love all humankind. The Lord invites us, through his own suffering, to unite with all those who are in pain and who are suffering various afflictions.

In accepting our own suffering we are able to understand the pain of others. Jesus walks in solidarity with every person on earth who is suffering. We have a God who is not afraid to be with the weak, the poor, and the vulnerable.

Passion (Palm) Sunday—Cycle A
Isaiah 50:4-7; Philippians 2:6-11; Matthew 26:14–27:66

Reflection: In the days ahead, I walk out to the Mount of Olives, the place where olives are crushed and made into oil. On the Mount of Olives I surrender my pain. I give it to the Lord that it might be crushed and made into something new, the oil of gladness, joy, peace, love, and compassion. Unless I accept my human condition with all its suffering, I cannot know the awesome power of God's compassion and love.

Ponder: Do I identify with anyone in the story of Jesus' passion? Peter? Judas? Mary Magdalene? the crowd? Jesus' mother? Pilate? Jesus himself? Am I apt to go along with the crowd? Do I identify with suffering? Am I compassionate when confronted with someone else's suffering?

Prayer: God, bless me with compassion. Help me to accept my suffering and surrender my pain to you.

Practice: This week I will fast from blaming others for their pains and afflictions; I will pray for greater self-control and perseverance; I will give a consoling embrace to someone who is suffering.

Cycle B
Anticipating Death in Love

"'She has done what she could. By perfuming my body she is anticipating its preparation for burial. I assure you, wherever the good news is proclaimed throughout the world, what she has done will be told in her memory'" (Mark 14:8-9).

Weeks ago, on Ash Wednesday, when we received the imprint of ashes on our foreheads, we were reminded of our need to die to selfishness and sin. Through that ritual we made a public commitment to reform our lives and believe wholeheartedly in the gospel, the Good News of Jesus Christ. Since then, we have sifted through the meaning of the ashes to find that we cannot ignore the reality of death; and we must all pass through this experience before we can know the glory of the Resurrection.

In the gospel an unnamed woman comes forward to anoint the body of Jesus with expensive oil. She probably purchased the oil in order to sell it as a means of income for herself. With great love for Jesus, she decides to break open the jar of oil and anoint the one she loves. The real anointing comes from the sanctuary of the woman's heart. Her love for the Lord is made manifest in the anointing. Her humble love becomes the authentic sign and symbol of what it means to be a person renewed and transformed in Christ. Of all the people that come to know Jesus and hear his message, this woman is the one who anticipates the death of Jesus with love. She wants to assure her beloved Lord that he can go to his death with the knowledge and experience that someone truly loved and respected him for what he did for the least ones.

During this week we embrace the reality of our own passion and death; we reflect more deeply on our own mortality. As followers of the Risen Lord we cannot separate ourselves from the passion experience that ultimately is a spiritual call to die for the sake of the kingdom of God.

As Christians we do the world a great service by walking in the spirit of love and kindness, anticipating the needs of our sisters and brothers, especially the poor and all those near death. Since we are all near death, it becomes a matter of great urgency that we do our best to break out of our selfish routines, open our hearts, and practice the healing ritual of love. It is not enough to receive ashes. We must be prepared to follow the Lord to the end. God has already prepared us for our death because we have been anointed in the love of our Lord and Savior, Jesus Christ.

Passion (Palm) Sunday—Cycle B
Isaiah 50:4-7; Philippians 2:6-11; Mark 14:1–15:47

Reflection: The woman in the gospel is not afraid to let go of her jar of expensive oil. She is not a selfish woman. She knows that there is something more precious and valuable to be obtained by showing love and kindness to someone who is about to experience death. Jesus does not want us to forget the woman in the gospel because he does not want us to forget how to prepare one another for that which lies beyond the experience of death: new life and peace.

Ponder: Am I ready and willing to let go of everything in order to possess the new and eternal life that God offers me through Christ? How attached am I to my possessions? my job? my family? my friends? life itself? Do I ever think about death? Am I afraid to die? What frightens me about death? Do I pray when I am afraid? Do I ask friends or family to pray with me when I am afraid?

Prayer: God, bless me with compassion. Help me to prepare for life beyond death.

Practice: This week I will fast from fear and denial of death; I will pray for the courage to meet death as a friend; I will give away a favorite possession.

Cycle C
The Table of Love

"When the hour arrived, Jesus took his place at table, and the apostles with him. He said to them: 'I have greatly desired to eat this Passover with you before I suffer. I tell you, I will not eat again until it is fulfilled in the kingdom of God'" (Luke 22:14-16).

It was customary for Jesus and the apostles to take their places at the table to eat and talk about their experiences. Jesus and his friends were more than a community; they were family. Every time Jesus and his friends ate together, they strengthened the bonds of love, friendship, and companionship. The ritual of being together and eating was important in the life and ministry of Jesus.

Just before his death, Jesus desires to eat one more time with those he has come to know, love, and serve. He is determined to give his friends one more example of unselfish love. He is anxious to get to his place at the table so he can tell his friends how much he truly loves them. He wants them to know and understand the importance of being together at the table and how the table creates community, heals broken hearts, resolves conflicts, and opens the way to peace. He desires one more opportunity to be at the table—the place of love.

In the breaking of the bread and the sharing of the cup, Jesus leaves us a profound and lasting message: "Love one another as I love you." Jesus breaks down all the barriers and walls that cause division and separation. He transcends the cultural, political, and social conflicts and tells the world that it's time to come together and eat as family and friends—for the kingdom of God is at hand.

Jesus tells his friends to remember what takes place at the table and to share the experience with others. In a much broader sense, Jesus desires to eat with people from all walks of life. Everyone is to be included in the celebration around the table of love. In the midst of personal pain and suffering, Jesus remains faithful to his mission of sharing the Good News of God's love.

In times of suffering, we need to be with people who know us and accept us as we are. We need to be in a community that is not afraid to invite us as sisters and brothers to take a place at the table. As followers of Christ, we believe that the kingdom of God is reflected each time we come together to listen to the Word of God, worship together, and join hands to serve the needs of all. The mission of gathering God's people together is not yet complete, however. There are many people in our community and throughout this world who need to know that someone cares about them and desires to be with them.

Passion (Palm) Sunday—Cycle C
Isaiah 50:4-7; Philippians 2:6-11; Luke 22:14–23:56

Reflection: I imagine a great table of love in the center of the world, with everyone having his or her own place at the table. It is time for me to reclaim that table of love and find a place around the Lord. After all, none of us can survive in this world without community, family, and friends. It is not enough for me to desire the kingdom of God; I must do my best to live the kingdom of God on earth. Perhaps this is what Jesus means when he says, "Do this in remembrance of me."

Ponder: What makes food such an important part of life? Do I enjoy eating a meal with friends or family? Is there anyone with whom I would not share a meal? What do I feed myself—physically, mentally, emotionally, and spiritually? Junk food? health food? Do I overeat—physically, mentally, emotionally, or spiritually? Do I starve myself—physically, mentally, emotionally, or spiritually? Is love a nourishing food? Have I been nourished with love? Do I nourish others with love?

Prayer: God, bless me with compassion. Help me to sit in community at your table of love.

Practice: This week I will fast from high risk behavior; I will pray for the gift of unselfish love; I will plan an ecumenical community supper to benefit the poor.

Monday of Holy Week
Isaiah 42:1-7; John 12:1-11

Reflection: I appreciate having someone rub my feet or scratch my back. I like having my hairdresser wash and cut my hair. I enjoy relaxing in a hot bath. I take comfort in warm, loving hugs. I feel grateful when I am sick and someone brings me something to drink or eat, or sits and talks with me. Yet sometimes I neglect my physical needs in favor of mental, emotional, or spiritual requirements; somehow the physical seems less important to me. I need to remember that loving care of my body demonstrates respect for this earthen vessel that houses my being, and that in order to be balanced and whole, my mental, emotional, spiritual, and physical aspects must all be in harmony.

Ponder: How do I feel when someone lovingly attends to my needs? Are my needs important? Do I ever attend to others' needs? Am I afraid to let people comfort me? Am I afraid to comfort others? Who are the poor around me? Do I consider myself one of the poor? What does "justice" mean to me?

Prayer: God, bless me with compassion. Help me to be a holy, integrated person.

Practice: Today I will fast from letting others take advantage of my goodness; I will pray for the integration of my mind, body, and spirit; I will take a tea or juice break when I am tired, and I will serve someone else who needs a break as well.

Tuesday of Holy Week
Isaiah 49:1-6; John 13:21-33,36-38

Reflection: God has called me by name to serve as my talents allow me. It is not always clear to what manner of service I am called, however, because I am not necessarily aware of the talents I have. I may have one talent; I may have dozens; I may be blocking my talents with fear of failure, fear of being used, fear of criticism. God calls me by name especially to be whole and to be loved. When I spend time with God asking for guidance, God teaches me to follow my instincts and my interests to uncover my talents. If I find I am apathetic, unmotivated, depressed, uncaring, or frozen by fear, God will give me the courage to seek out a caring friend who can help me.

    Ponder: What ae my interests? What talents do I use in God's service? Am I afraid to use my talents for the good of others? Does God ask anything of me that I cannot handle?

Prayer: God, bless me with compassion. Help me to recognize and use the gifts within me.

Practice: Today I will fast from remaining unmotivated; I will pray for a spirit of loving service; I will find a concrete way to serve others in the community: setting up for an event, selling tickets, posting flyers, sitting in the audience.

Wednesday of Holy Week
Isaiah 50:4-9; Matthew 26:14-25

Reflection: Selfishness, greed, resentment, envy, prejudice, dishonesty, disloyalty, discrimination, arrogance, rudeness, self-righteousness, vengeance: these are examples of the ways I betray God, myself, and others.

Ponder: Do I use God's gifts in God's service? What prompts me to rebel against God? Pride? selfishness? arrogance? Have I ever betrayed another person? Have I ever betrayed myself? Have I ever betrayed God? Are there times I am like Judas?

Prayer: God, bless me with compassion. Help me to express my love and appreciation for others.

Practice: Today I will fast from telling lies; I will pray for a spirit of selflessness; I will tell someone "I am sorry."

Holy Thursday
Exodus 12:1-8,11-14; 1 Corinthians 11:23-26; John 13:1-15

Reflection: I like being in charge because I like telling others what to do. I like to do the things that bring me recognition and to leave the boring, mundane details for others to do. Jesus shows me, however, that true leadership does not depend on being recognized or important: true leadership is service to others. The more willing I am to serve others, the less self-centered I become. When I reach out to the poor, the lonely, the afraid, the abused, or the neglected, I practice the way of compassion, understanding, peace, and love. This is the kind of servant God calls me to be.

Ponder: When do I remember Jesus? Do I approach the table of the Lord with joy? Do I serve others? Do I let others serve me? Am I a willing servant of God?

Prayer: God, bless me with compassion. Help me to be a humble servant.

Practice: Today I will fast from self-importance; I will pray for the willingness to serve; I will become involved in a service project in my community.

Good Friday
Isaiah 52:13–53:12; Hebrews 4:14-16; 5:7-9; John 18:1–19:42

Reflection: Surrender is a gift I freely give; it is not something taken from me. Surrender empties me of the human sins of pride, fear, shame, anger, and self-righteousness. Surrender fills me with God's love, compassion, peace, serenity, joy, and glory. Surrender permits me to follow God's path without struggle. Surrender empowers me to emanate God's word and love from my being.

Ponder: What is my concept of God's kingdom? How eager am I to surrender to God's will? Can I relate to Jesus the King as he hangs dying on the cross? Do I feel crucified by others? Do I feel Mary's pain and anguish? Whom have I "condemned"?

Prayer: God, bless me with compassion. Help me to surrender all that I am to you.

Practice: Today I will fast from disobedience; I will pray for a spirit of surrender; I will eat only one simple meal.

Holy Saturday

Exodus 14:15-15:1; Romans 6:3-11
Cycle A: Matthew 28:1-10
Cycle B: Mark 16:1-8
Cycle C: Luke 24:1-12

Reflection: The media are always spreading news of violence, disaster, deprivation, war, disease, tragedy, and death. When I feed only on this kind of news, I feel depressed, hopeless, and pessimistic. I need to consciously look for positive, affirming news of compassion, love, and peace in the world. There are many examples in my own community and my own family if I choose to look for them: someone who runs an errand for a busy parent; someone who visits a homebound person; someone who picks up litter off the sidewalk; someone who smiles when walking by; someone who listens to another's problems. Works of compassion, love, and peace are usually simple, seldom newsworthy. Part of my responsibility as a Christian is to bring the news to others that God is simple, God is love.

Ponder: What kind of news am I in a hurry to share? Do I hurry to share the news of Jesus' Resurrection? Do I share more bad news than good news? How does any news affect me?

Prayer: God, bless me with compassion. Help me to live with hope.

Practice: Today I will fast from pessimism; I will pray for hope; I will share only positive, hopeful news with others.

Easter

Cycle A
From Darkness to Light

"Early in the morning on the first day of the week, while it was still dark, Mary Magdalene came to the tomb. She saw that the stone had been moved away…" (John 20:1).

Jesus is risen! He is to be found alive in our hearts. We are no longer children of darkness but children of light. We live convinced by our faith in the God of love that we are God's handiwork on earth. With the Risen Christ we are called to bring the Good News of hope, peace, and reconciliation into the world where people desperately need to hear about and experience the Resurrection.

In the Risen Jesus, we are given a new awareness of God, our neighbor, and ourselves. We are more aware of God's presence and action in our lives. We are aware of the hope that is to be found in the trust that God has not abandoned us but truly walks with us even in the darkest moments of life.

In the Risen Jesus, we are not afraid to enter into relationship with people from different backgrounds. We are eager to resolve our conflicts, to respect differences, to refrain from judging others, and to show compassion to the least of our sisters and brothers.

In the Risen Jesus, we take seriously our responsibility to confront the darkness of selfishness, greed, and power with the light of selflessness, generosity, and humble service. We are committed to be the countercultural signs of justice and peace in the midst of opposing forces.

Sometimes we prefer to stay in the tomb, thinking that we are safe and secure. To be a Christian witness in the world, however, is to leave the tomb of safety and security and to take on the risk of being misunderstood and rejected in a pluralistic society. Without losing the light of hope and peace, we do our best to patiently understand that God's loving kindness is the only way to tear down the walls of resistance to change.

The Risen Jesus has broken through the darkness and shines as the light of love and peace in our world. May the light in our hearts show others the way to this everlasting peace.

Easter Sunday—Cycle A
Acts 10:34,26-43; 1 Corinthians 5:6-8; John 20:1-9

Reflection: After consciously living with Jesus for the last six weeks, I now live a new life with a positive attitude, a renewed spirituality, and a better understanding of myself, God, and my neighbor. Because Jesus is risen, a whole new world of possibilities is open before me. I can now bring about justice and peace; I can show compassion to the suffering; I can live in peace with people from all walks of life.

Ponder: Do I run to share the Good News with my friends? Do I believe that Jesus has been raised from the dead? Do I believe that I will be raised from the dead? Do I believe that God's light is in me?

Prayer: God of love, let me live in your light of hope and peace.

Practice: In light of the Easter event, I will continue to fast from selfishness and greed; I will continue to pray for selflessness and generosity; I will continue to offer humble service to those in need.

Cycle B
Jesus Alive in Us

"And very early on the first day of the week, when the sun had risen, they went to the tomb. They had been saying to one another, 'Who will roll away the stone for us from the entrance to the tomb?' When they looked up, they saw that the stone, which was very large, had already been rolled back" (Mark 16:2-4).

Nothing is impossible with God. The stone is rolled back from the entrance of the tomb, and Jesus walks out of the cold, dark place of death and into new life. There is no fanfare, no marching band, no parade, no major pronouncement, no news coverage. In the quiet of the morning, the Risen Lord empowers the world with compassion, love, and peace. Jesus comes out of the tomb for all those to whom he promised new life and hope.

The Resurrection of Jesus is not just a story; it is the event of God's love that continues to reshape the emotional, spiritual, mental, and social landscape of people's lives. Through the Resurrection of Jesus, God affirms the gift of life. Through Christ, God shows us that the journey of life does not end with death; it merely changes and becomes a new reality. This new life is not something we can create at will; rather it is given to us as a sign of God's great love. The new life that God promises is, in one sense, already within us through faith. The Risen Lord can be found in the inner sanctuary of our hearts, and from this sacred space Jesus continues to fill the world with love, compassion, peace, and hope. We have been given a special power to reshape and change the world.

Easter is the time for us to become more aware of the Risen Lord already living within us. It is the time to believe in the truth that we can change the way we think and act in the world. We can roll back the stone of hatred and experience genuine love. We can roll back the stone of despair and embrace the spirit of hope. We can roll back the stone of selfishness and share the gift of compassion with the poor and brokenhearted. We can roll back the stone of disbelief and rediscover our roots with God and in God.

If we are sincerely interested in finding the Lord, we need only look into our hearts. When we begin to see the light of the Resurrection of Jesus in ourselves, we can rejoice and be glad. We can run and share the Good News that Jesus is alive in us.

As people of the Resurrection, we give witness to the inner meaning of this event of God. In essence, we make every effort to affirm life, to be peacemakers, to share in the suffering and pain of others, to be bearers of hope, and to be open to the movement of the Spirit of the Lord.

Easter Sunday—Cycle B
Acts 10:34,37-43; 1 Corinthians 5:6-8; Mark 16:1-8
(from the Easter Vigil)

Reflection: I do not live in the cold, dark place of death. Rather I walk out of the tomb with Jesus and embrace the new life that is offered in love. I bring the news of Jesus' Resurrection to new places and seize every opportunity to empower the world with compassion, love, and peace. All things are indeed possible because I believe in my heart that Jesus is alive in me. I will never tire of bringing this Good News to my sisters and brothers next door and around the world.

Ponder: What huge stones block the entrance to my heart? Greed? despair? depression? low self-esteem? prejudice? resentment? addictions? Am I willing to roll back these stones? Do I want a new life of love, peace, and compassion—for myself and others? Do I believe that Jesus is alive in me? With Jesus alive in me, how am I empowered?

Prayer: God of love, let me live in your light of compassion and new life.

Practice: In light of the Easter event, I will continue to fast from hatred and despair; I will continue to pray for love and faith; I will continue to affirm human life in all its diverse forms.

Cycle C
Making Sense Out of Nonsense

"The other women with them also told the apostles, but the story seemed like nonsense and they refused to believe them" (Luke 24:10-11).

The apostles just cannot believe the story because they cannot see beyond the nonsense of their culture which characterizes women as second-class citizens and unreliable sources of information. The women cannot possibly have been chosen by God to be the bearers of Good News, the news that Jesus is risen from the tomb as promised.

We cannot underestimate the wisdom of God and the many ways in which the message of the Resurrection is passed on in the world. God speaks to us in ways that are usually beyond our control and imagination. We are constantly being surprised into new understandings of God and are forced to see with new eyes, to feel with new hearts, to listen with new ears, and to connect with new hands.

The Resurrection of Jesus is a countercultural event; it is something that catches people off guard; it is something totally unexpected. In fact, some people thought the Resurrection would actually never take place. Even those closest to Jesus had a difficult time believing the promise.

The Risen Jesus helps us become more aware of what lies beyond our immediate world; he gives us a new vision of life when life makes the least amount of sense. The Risen Jesus shows us the power of hope when we are lost in the nonsense of discouragement and indifference. The Risen Jesus convinces us that love is stronger than death, especially when we are overwhelmed with the nonsense of war and violence, abuse and neglect. The Risen Jesus heals and reconciles a world caught up in the nonsense of racism, prejudice, and hatred. The Risen Jesus gives us a deeper sense of God's kingdom of love and peace.

Today Jesus invites us to look for the story of the Resurrection where we least expect to find hope and peace. We are asked to take the risk to hear God speaking through the poor, the brokenhearted, the sick, and the suffering around us. As we look beneath the surface of human weakness, we will find the mystery of the cross: the death and resurrection of the Lord. We will also uncover a new sense and purpose for living in the world.

Easter Sunday—Cycle C
Acts 10:34,37-43; 1 Corinthians 5:6-8; Luke 24:1-12
(from the Easter Vigil)

Reflection: Jesus experiences the cross; he suffers; he dies; he is risen from the dead. Jesus does all this to remind me that God is with me on my life's journey. I am but a pilgrim here on this earth. I am not going to live here forever, for my real home is beyond this world. Until I reach my true destiny, I am given the privilege to walk in the light and hope of the Resurrection of Jesus, a new reality that helps me make sense out of nonsense. I carry within myself a sense of the sacred, a sense of peace, a sense of love. The story of the Resurrection surrounds me and begs me to listen with a renewed mind and heart. I am with the women who go to the empty tomb and bring the astonishing news of God's love to the world: Jesus Christ is risen!

Ponder: Is there anything in my life that doesn't make sense? Illness? abuse? unemployment? loss of a loved one? Do I know that God loves me? Do I believe that God loves me? Do I trust that the light and hope of the Resurrection can make sense out of the nonsense in my life? Am I willing to share the Good News of God's love and peace in the world?

Prayer: God of love, let me live in your light of healing and reconciliation.

Practice: In light of the Easter event, I will continue to fast from discouragement and indifference; I will continue to pray for hope and compassion; I will continue to share my gifts and talents wherever they are needed.

Special Feast Days During Lent

Chair of Peter
February 22
1 Peter 5:1-4; Matthew 16:13-19

Reflection: When I focus on another person's life, habits, or problems, I am usually afraid to focus on my own. When I find myself talking about someone else's problems; when I find myself prying into someone else's business; when I find myself making mental lists of things wrong with other people; when I find myself gossiping about other people: I can be sure that my mind is avoiding something about myself that I need to examine. I need to ask God to bless me with the willingness to take my focus off other people's lives and put it on my own so that I let go of all the obstacles that prevent me from loving myself, God, and my neighbor.

Ponder: Do I focus on other people's problems more than my own? Is my life a model of loving kindness? Am I afraid to look at my own life and see what I need to change? What obstacles prevent me from loving myself, God, and my neighbor?

Prayer: God, lead me on the path of your light. Help me to focus on what I need to change in my life.

Practice: Today I will fast from talking about others; I will pray for self-discipline; I will not criticize people.

Feast of Saint Joseph
March 19
2 Samuel 7:4-5,12-14,16; Romans 4:13,16-18,22; Luke 2:41-51

Reflection: The faith I have in God's mercy and loving kindness allows me to pray for healing and forgiveness because I know that God will never turn away from me. I am the one who turns away from God by choosing attitudes that are unjust, unkind, or unloving; I separate myself from God's love and end up hurting myself and others. Love is what connects me to my sisters and brothers, and without this love I lose touch with God.

Ponder: Do I allow God to correct my mistakes? Do I have faith enough to ask for correction? What makes faith essential in my relationship with God? Do my human relationships need more faith? more trust? more compassion? more willingness to admit my mistakes?

Prayer: God, heal my blindness. Open my eyes to see your mercy and love.

Practice: Today I will fast from unjust and unkind thoughts and feelings; I will pray for faith; I will choose an attitude of love in my interactions with others.

Annunciation of the Lord
March 25
Isaiah 7:10-14; 8:10; Hebrews 10:4-10; Luke 1:26-38

Reflection: I am afraid of many things: getting lost when I travel somewhere new; snarling dogs; other people's anger aimed at me; being unloved; drunken behavior; gangs of people; making mistakes; dying. Yet, the fears lose their power over me as I learn to name them and as I learn to trust in God's unconditional love for me. Learning to trust in God's love becomes easier the more I turn my life and will over to God: I know that God leads me the way I need to go. No pain, no trauma, no crisis, has the power to dominate me when I walk in God's path.

Ponder: Is God with me today? Where can I find God? Am I afraid to do God's will? What fears block me? Can I name them? How am I a servant of the Lord?

Prayer: God, show me the spirit of your life within me so that I may live without fear.

Practice: Today I will fast from fear; I will pray for inner strength; I will visit someone who is afraid to be alone.